Francis Keene

Bella Moon

Poetry for Children

Emerald Sea books

Bella Moon

This book is respectfully dedicated to my two sons, who know how to close their eyes and dream a while.

CONTENTS

THE GOOD MANNERS OF CATS

She lived in a castle with 400 rooms.
In her parlor she resided for high tea at noon.

She shuffled her feet at a sensible pace,
In a Victorian gown made of Chantilly lace.

Her cheeks were all ruddy and her eyes twinkled blue,
When each day she prepared the same dinner of stew.

As she laid out the bowls, one would heartily exclaim,
"Why there's 900 bowls—is this possibly sane?"

She smiled, delighted, as she ladled each meal,
And each cat waited patiently for his or her fill.

The older and wisest cats, Lola and May,
Gathered 12 kittens to help for the day.

You might think serving 900 cats is a feat,
But surprised you would be when they sit down to eat.

First they form a straight line, then march deftly in pairs,
All through the halls, then down all the stairs.

Into the dining hall, not to be late,
They're seated in time to eat dinner at eight.

The silverware is set and napkins laid apart,

And the table is where all good manners must start.

The older, more dainty cats always sit first;
The gentle-cats follow as the kittens disperse.

All is order—not mayhem—so courteous and polite,
And when all are seated, 'tis indeed a great sight.

The cats fold their paws to show how they care,
So gracious in manner expressing their prayer.

"Please pass me the pepper," said respectfully, 'twould seem.
"Please pass me my saucer to drink all my cream."

When dinner is eaten, the elders sit tight,
For the kittens are tired and must bid their goodnight.

And the Victorian woman sighs contentedly this eve,
For once again all was order,
As the cats took their leave.

DOGS, OH DOGS

I want a dog, but which is best?
Let's put our knowledge to the test.

A poodle is small, with hair that's curly,
While pugs and bulldogs are big and burly.

Siberian huskies, I've heard it said,
Work hard in snow by pulling sleds.

Fox and coonhounds, a few to name,
Are breeds of hounds that hunt for game.

The German shepherd or collie I'd keep
If I were a farmer herding sheep.

To a golden retriever or cocker spaniel,
I'd give a name like Duke or Daniel.

A fearless watchdog, that's what I need.
There's the Irish, Welsh, of the terrier breed.

But which to choose, I haven't a clue,
So I'll leave that decision up to you!

THE MAGICAL EVE

Rapture is far too close, I hear,
For Christmas Eve is drawing near.

Feasts shall tempt with unearthly sights
Of honeyed hams and sweet delights.

Yorkshire pudding, butter-cream sweets,
Sugarplums, gumdrops—my favorite treats.

Those warm and cozy toasty nights,
With blazing fires and flickering lights.

Enchanted carols drift close and gay,
As Santa's elves work night and day.

Wrappings, ribbons, tinsel, holly—
Santa's elves watch children's folly.

Christmas jingles angels sing,
What we have wished, may Santa bring.

When stardust twinkles, and the moon shines bright,
'It's Santa's reindeer taking flight.

Listen closely, gaze with wonder,
For Santa's sleigh bells sound like thunder.

Now as you close your sleepy eyes,

Santa glides through winter skies.

And the magic stays alive, if you believe
In the spirit of Santa on Christmas Eve.

JORDY JOOPER

Jordy Jooper was a pest,
Hurtling cheese balls at my vest.

Plucking, flinging slimy balls—
Slipping, sliding down the halls.

Jordy Jooper likes to holler.
Yodeling, yelling like a bawler.

"Jordy Jooper, won't you quit—
Detention hall is where you'll sit!"

He'd kick, he'd hit, without a care,
With no regard for what was fair.

Peanut-butter-jelly wars
With pride he'd start in corridors.

"School, oh School—I will not go,
With Jordy Jooper as my foe!"

I'd cry, I'd crumple in a ball—
My feet would shuffle down the hall.

One day I knew I'd take a stand,
And squarely, squirrely where I'd land.

And then I knew the answer clearly—

Exactly how he'd start to fear me.

A super hero is what I needed—
I begged, I yelled, I super-pleaded!

I raised my fist up to the sky.
I need a hero type of guy!

Then crashing! Boom! Ahoy! It splattered!
Crusty tinsel tin all tattered.

A spaceship landed on the lawn,
And in a flash Jordy was gone!

But then it was just so peculiar,
What would become of him next school year.

Why Jordy Jooper beside me walked—
All please and thank yous when he talked.

Reciting all his four plus threezes,
Jeenxy jibs—no longer teases.

Giant Jupiter, I'm so GLAD
That Jordy Jooper is no longer BAD!

THE TOURNAMENT

The king sat down,
With his queen on his right,
Away from their duties
To enjoy the courtly fight.

Shining armor,
Glowing with pride;
Horses prancing
Side by side.

Honesty and truth set aside for the game,
While the gallant knights ride for their glorious fame.

The knights at last
Un-shield their masks.

Knights of horse,
Knights of war—
The round table empty of knights, no more.

Knightly honor, tried and true,
Has lost the game
For now—it's through.

THE FAIRY QUEEN MATILDA

The fairy queen Matilda
Gazed through her looking glass
And found to her dismay
A wicked spell had been cast.

"Oh me, oh my, good gracious,"
She delicately exclaimed,
"For who has caused this mischief,
And who shall be to blame?"

She sighed, a trifle weary,
Then began her mysterious chant:
"Oh, Bluebells, sing so merry—
Please summon all my fairies."

From lands afar, they fluttered
As twinkles in the night,
And all the while, they muttered
As they were taking flight.

"Oh, Bluebells, sing so merry.
Come hither from your land.
Oh wild, mystic Bluebells,
Bring forth your magic sand."

The dulcet little Bluebells
At once expressed their dire,
"It's the wicked witch from Jagged Cliffs,

With eyes that blaze like fire.

She's the wicked witch beguile,
With a mean, diabolical smile.
As she awaits the helpless who tarry,
She casts spells so wickedly merry.

She turned our sand to stone,
Then captured all our treasure,
And all the while she cackled,
So mirthless in her pleasure."

The Fairy Queen Matilda,
Without a bit of dread,
Did listen quite intently,
And this is what she said:

"It's good tidings that I bring thee
Of news I must foretell.
Alas, do listen closely
To break the wicked spell.

'Twould take two mortal children
To gaze upon the skies
With great imagination
And dreamy, wondrous eyes."

The fairies fell to silence
To gaze upon the stone,
And knew they must abruptly
Restore their fairy throne.

But the years did pass quite slowly,
While many children passed
Upon the land of stone and ice,
But still the spell held fast.

The stone began to crumble,
The ice began to thaw,
Yet still no child dared to dream
Of mythical lands with awe.

The wicked witch of Jagged Cliffs
Began to plant her seeds
Of gnarled roots and crooked limbs
That sprouted quick as weeds.

But deep within the gnarled woods,
'Twas there that lived a boy,
With eyes as blue as the summer skies
And a heart that sang with joy.

Though he was poor with scarcely a crumb,
'Twas not the matter at hand,
For he lived for adventure, and no one could quell
His spirit for exploring the land.

One day he wandered through the woods
And came upon the stone,
Imagining at once an ancient castle
With a golden prince's throne.

Thereafter each day he did return

And saw to his delight
A bonnie lass with emerald eyes
And locks as black as night.

At once he sauntered to the lass
To acquaint her with his name.
"They call me Jamie, bonnie lass—
Come now, let's play a game.

The stone is my castle,
The ice is your sea,
And the woods are the kingdom
That forever shall be."

The bonnie lass, whose name was Claire,
With blushing cheeks as fair as fair,
Had stolen young Jamie's tender heart
And vowed to never be apart.

Now the fairies, eager from their glee,
Sat down for crumpets with their tea,
And the Bluebells sang with great delight
Throughout this day and into night.

The sun shone bright on this mystical day,
For the wicked spell was cast away.
And the Fairy Queen Matilda sighed,
For the wicked witch had been defied.

As the stone transformed to sparkling sand,
The ice changed to both sea and land,

And Claire and Jamie, side by side,
Looked to the fairies as their guide.

For here they'd rule,
Once they grew and married,
As King and Queen
Of this land of fairies.

And the fairies taught them how to rule
By sending them to fairy school.
And this is what the fairies said
Each night they tucked them into bed:

"Oh, children, dream of fairy land
And doors that stand ajar,
For through those doors, you shall traverse
To mythical lands afar."

THE CATERPILLAR

"How came you here,
Mr. CATERpillar, dear?"

"I slithered and tithered,"
He mumbled with fright.
"My journey was far
As I marched through the night!"

"The tall redwood forest
Is where you are now.
Go hide beneath leaves
And stay hidden somehow."

"For now I must eat
So my body can molt.
Please watch where you step—
Or you'll give me a jolt!"

"Alas, CATERpillar,
For here you must stay,
Until morning comes
And turns darkness to DAY."

As silent as sound
Was the caterpillar's sleep.
And back to his log
Was where Mr. Frog leaped.

"And so with a sigh,
I must bid you goodbye."
And he thanked Mr. Frog
As a new BUTTERFLY!

WAKE UP, EASTER!

Winter's sleep
Springtime's call
Blooming meadows
Raindrops fall—

Easter's come to all.

EASTER DREAMS

Sugar dusted rainbows
Flowing chocolate streams
Sleepy children rise,
Awake for Easter dreams!

COUSIN BILLY'S NOODLE GOO!

My silly cousin Billy
Ties noodles in his hair
And thinks he looks quite dandy
When people gawk and stare.

His hairdo's slick and sticky
From clingy noodle junk.
It springs up like Medusa
From gluey noodle gunk.

His teacher tried to tell him,
"Clean up your noodle goo!"
But silly cousin Billy
Has better things to do.

Like cook gluey goo-noodles,
All purple, green, and blue,
Cause when he acts quite silly,
He'll paste them straight on you.

When Billy meets new people,
He doesn't shake their hands,
But flings flimsy goo-noodles
And laughs at where they land!

His Granny always tells him,
"Now, Billy, just you quit!"
But silly cousin Billy

Won't listen—not one bit!

And so I must forewarn you,
Steer clear of Billy, too.
Just run away quite madly,
Or get struck with noodle goo!

TURTLE TUTTLES

Little Turtle Tuttles,
Chatting as he scuttles,
Singing how he's lucky
To the baby ducky.

NESTING IN THE TREE

Look at the nest
Up in the tree—
Ever wonder how it came to be?

Birds gather their twigs all day long,
While building and singing their beautiful song.

CHIRP! CHIRP!

Chirping crickets
Chat at night,
Making noise
From dusk 'til light.

Chirp! Chirp! Chirp!

SPRING'S RAINDROP

Hold a raindrop in your hand.
Watch it vanish in the sand.

See the raindrop melt away.
Feel it in the ocean spray.

See the raindrop feed the flower—
Thank the raindrop for its power.

BABY BLUE EYES

Baby, baby blue eyes,
Cooing gentle lullabies.
Make those rain clouds go away,
And bring me back a sunny day.

THE QUIET-TIME HOUSE

Shhh . . . hushhh . . . it's the quite-time house.
It's time to rest.
It's quiet time.

Lay your head down.
Rest a while.

Shhh . . . the quiet-time house is resting now—

The couch

The lamp

The fuzzy rug

The teddy bear

The puppy

And the kittens are all sleeping now.

It's time for peace
It's time to rest
It's time to shhh

In the quiet-time house.

COLOR THE FESTIVAL BRIGHT

Melting snow trickles . . . A   W   A   Y
Flowing streams SWELL
Snowy mountains thaw
Water rushes D
          O
        W
           N
Sunshine radiates . . . L O N G E R
     Springing forth
Y
                     Daisies and Rose Angels blossom
K
                        Reaching gently towards the
S
Gophers awaken
Scampering about
Misty raindrops, muddy puddles
Sour cherries and dandelions

     Color the festival bright

Springtime is here!

ABOUT THE AUTHOR

Francis Keene lives in the Pacific Northwest with her husband, two sons, and white fluffy dog. You can email her at Keene.Francis@comcast.net.

67205600R00021

Made in the USA
Middletown, DE
19 March 2018